T0195933

STEP
INTO YOUR
SHOES

YOUR JOURNEY
IS WELL WORTH IT

MADELINE BELL

BALBOA.PRESS
A DIVISION OF HAY HOUSE

Balboa Press books may be ordered through booksellers or by contacting:

Balboa Press
A Division of Hay House
1663 Liberty Drive
Bloomington, IN 47403
www.balboapress.com
1 (877) 407-4847

Print information available on the last page.

ISBN: 978-1-9822-4152-0 (sc)
ISBN: 978-1-9822-4154-4 (hc)
ISBN: 978-1-9822-4153-7 (e)

Library of Congress Control Number: 2020901557

Balboa Press rev. date: 01/21/2020

To my husband, John

"There you are"

Contents

Why I wrote this book

For a lifetime, I have lived with guards up. My guard was up because while growing up, when I would open up my true self, at times, I faced ridicule. My ideas mattered so long as I did as others wanted me to do, thought like others wanted me to think, pursued what others needed and expected me to pursue, which was not much as a Latin girl. I took the ridicules and walked, what felt alone, in my shoes. With decades behind me of walking in my shoes, I finally arrived at a place surrounded by love and acceptance, only to arrive and not recognize love and acceptance. I was lost in an unrecognizable foreign land.

In the beginning, I thought, I wrote this book only to share a story. I know now, it was more to realize that my shoes have brought me to a place full of much more love and acceptance that I could recognize and what I learned along the way is what I need to share. I had spent so much time fending off non-supporters that I had a difficult time recognizing the authentic supporters that I had rallied up around me. For some time, it was difficult for me to recognize my authentic supporters because they came to me from so many different perspectives and each are very much unique. As unique as each one of us is on this planet. When you are born and bred to simulate but cannot clam the cry of your inner voice, it is difficult to accept the uniqueness of the love that others have to offer you.

My shoes, the shoes that led me to this bliss, I had to remove. It is time to step into my new season shoes and begin walking in the love to which I have arrived. My journey is not over. I am now starting to learn to walk in the light which I have worked so hard to reach. Today, I am thankful for my new-found strength and for the ones that stood by me through this journey. Every bump, every wall, every tear, every moment, every step in my shoes. It has all been worth the love that surrounds me today that I now walk in my new season shoes ready to receive.

Sometimes I think I am ready for my life to be simple once again. In my shoes, to me, my life has not been difficult. For those around me, baring witness, it has been difficult for them.

Stay true to your shoes and all the right people and opportunities will enter your life. Some faces will be familiar, and some will be new. All will be great because all are presented to you for the reason that makes you, you. Being you is a great person to be. For if you are not you, then you cannot be. Step into your shoes with love. Walk your best self, every day, with pride and confidence. I hope this book helps you step in your journey and know that, someone does understand.

Introduction

Over twenty years ago the thought of writing a book entered my heart. I wanted to share some of what I have learned over the course of my journey while stepping in my shoes. I believe that through of all my many challenging experiences I was never alone. It was 1998 when the urge of sharing my story entered my heart. The internet was new. One day while waiting for my dial-up to connect to the internet, I felt my world begin to widen. The possibility of being able to reach out to others, connect with others, and stop my lonely aching mind became visible in my horizon.

I have started well over a dozen attempts at writing a book over the years. After writing a few chapters, my voice became lost in what I thought was the proper way to write. Taking an approach to conform to traditional writing styles, did not have enough authenticity for me. This frustrated me and my frustration kept me from continuing to write. So, I would stop, take a Zen moment, continued in my life, and when I came across inspiration again, I would try again. I went through this cycle dozens of times. Starting, stopping, and walking away, thinking I needed to educate myself more on how to write and believing timing was just not right.

During this time, I entered a season of my life where I experienced being coached to repress what was real in my life. Encouraged to conform to a world that I was working and studying so hard to claim my place in. A place where I knew my mine's capabilities and my work ethic would add value. I have worked for and met people that developed opinions of me based on what they saw on the surface. Statistics, pieces of data, and not the strengths that laid in my core. This is what it felt like. It also felt as if not much consideration was given that not everyone carries crosses based on ill choices. Repress, lie, and conform so others could be comfortable, were the messages I received in this season of my life, if I wished to progress in my career. I was coached to take measures to not make anyone uncomfortable to be around anything they have been lucky enough in life not to have experienced. I understood not to air out dirty laundry, but I could not deny the fact that I was a teenage mom and this fact did make some very uncomfortable.

Some people would tell me if I wanted to grow and be respected in my career, I needed to create an alternative story of this fact about me that I could be "proud" to chat about. But I was already proud of all that I have done and was doing.

I was not successful at creating these stories of fiction that would please others. How could I create a story that would hide the fact that I became a mom at 16? Also, I had no idea what components created a life story that others would be comfortable believing and comfortable being close to. And where was the consideration of my comfortableness in this message? In my shoes, I was unable to find the inspiration needed to create and tell stories that benefited others just because my true story either made others uncomfortable or, even worse, have them make terrible assumptions about me and my character.

I find strength in knowing that I discovered my shoes and stepped into my shoes long ago. Long before this season of my life. I am good within myself because of the value I place in my shoes.

Experiences such as these provide me opportunity to further recognize my shoes and not to fault my steps. The circumstances of my life are not unfortunate. Others, who do not experience such, may choose to believe this, but their belief does not make it so. Instead, I believe and hold firmly, that I am strong. I hold a brilliant vision that my unfortunate circumstances have provided me. It is this vision that I will share with you, in this book. There may be rocks in the path of a journey. Large rocks are worth standing on. They are not worth being avoided or discounted.

The difficult things that you overcome and continue to come across in your path as you step and walk in your shoes are the strongest part of the foundation that makes you, you. When you work hard to build a future for yourself, see these rocks that you must step to overcome as a solid foundation, one that jealous naysayers only wish they could build their house on.

Step in your shoes, regardless of the rocks and even large boulders you may come across. Here, in this book, I will share with you some of what I have learned from the rocks and boulders of my journey. One of these rock/boulders of mine is me working to get this book to you. I am terrible at writing grammatically correct, but that does not mean that I do not have important messages to share.

So many years of starts and stops of trying to get a book out to you. To share with you that "someone does understand", I failed because I placed so much focus on trying to be absolute with being grammatically correct with my writing. I did so even with this book and that was not going so well. So instead of asking for permission that all is just right in my writing, I am asking for forgiveness, upfront, for any grammatically incorrect writing you may encounter in reading my words to you. Although, please know, I have tried to clean up as best as I can.

The world needs "The possibilities of your capabilities", that you hold deep in your heart.

If, when you think of the possibilities of your capabilities, the vision in your mind has a difficult time forming what it considers to be a realistic path for you to follow, step in your shoes, and walk anyway. Believe. Step. Walk.

One quote that resonates with me was spoken by Henry Ford. He said, "Whether you think you can, or you think you can't -- you're right." Step into your shoes and start believing that you can, because you are right, you can. The world will see you as you see yourself. Step into your shoes and walk your journey. The visions that your heart draws you towards are visions that your mind may not be able to conceptualize today. If this is true for you, step into your shoes and journey on. Your path holds the light you seek.

This is my first attempt at writing and completing anything for publish and I admit, it is FAR from perfect. I want to speak to you. I hope for you to hear my voice and to get to know me. I want to connect with you and you to connect with someone that does understand. If anything in this book helps you in anyway, I would be thrilled.

This book is not without imperfection from a formally grammatical perspective or structured writing styles. But here you will find my authentic voice speaking to you. I am educated in accounting and computer systems. I know how to bridge gaps. This is my productive wheel house. It is what I do, and I am darn good at this and much more.

I have also come up and have become a part of a change that my upbringing cannot deny. I am blessed to recognize that I have landed in a place where the world is beginning to recognize untapped talent. My talent. Your talent. Step into your shoes. The world needs us. I am blessed to have survived and be part of this movement. What I do not know and am not blessed with is grammar and proper writing styles. But, regardless, I have still made every self-attempt to make this legible. I smile here.

I am pursuing this writing hurdle mostly on my own and have decided to publish this book with any and all my faults, which I am sure you will come across as you read. But after trying for months to pursue assistance with this grave imperfection of mine and not being successful in obtaining this assistance, I decided I was not going to let that stop me from getting my message to you, which is...

"Step into your shoes" and "Someone does understand"

In the end…I only have two wishes for this book.

One: I wish to let you know that "someone does understand" how much noise there is in the world and

Two: I wish for you to "Step into your shoes".

Someone does understand

First, I confess, I am not a licensed professional counselor of any kind. The only license that I hold is a Certified Public Accountant (CPA) license, which hardly qualifies me as any kind of therapist or philosopher. I write my words solely based on my experiences. There have been many moments in my life where I have asked God why He felt the need to show me and have me experience so many lessons or events that I believed were harsh and filled me with heartache and pain. Many times, the pain that these lessons or events caused me felt so unbearable at the time, they took my breathe away. Later, I realized that God had nothing to do with my pain. Rather, my pain, at times, was directed related to my choices, even if I had no intention, when making the decision, to make my life more difficult. No matter how long ago a choice is made or the innocence that I held, there were consequences; and God remains in my life to help see me through any such consequences, as He does for us all.

For most my life, I carried a cheap notebook and I would write. I did not write a journal. I just wrote because writing is what I did to keep myself, well I do not know. Perhaps grounded, preoccupied, or just to quiet the noise in my mind. The truth is, writing gave me an excuse to seek quiet moments where I could just keep to myself and escape. Something I have always needed. At one point in my writing I found myself trying to write poems. One day while writing, my final thought I wrote on the last page of my book, that I was carrying at the time, my final insertion read,

"…just so you know, that someone does understand…".

I am so sad that this steno book is currently lost. That was about 1992. That one passage I created has stayed with me. I did not write it to the world. I believe those words came to me because I needed to know that *someone does understand*. Enlightenment is what those words gave me. My inner voice speaking to me. The one voice that knows me and always has. My voice was telling me, even though "that someone" was not there in front of me, not within my arm's reach or any other type of reach, that no matter my circumstance, I was not alone in what I was experiencing. Not then not now, not ever. Someone out there does understand. Someone, somewhere, has been there, or is there, at the very same place, experiencing what I was.

What a powerful vision. What a gift I was given! A knowing and a place where I could breathe, deep and free. I am worthy. You are worthy. We all are worthy and not one of us are ever alone. Just breathe.

Those words, that came to me with no thought while I wrote in my steno book, changed my mine's eye. Those words provide me with comfort, then and still do so today. They give me breath. A breath I can take in deep. This ability to breathe in deep feels good and comforts me. This comfort has always been there for me whenever I need it most and when I remember to reflect on it. For a lifetime, I have lived with my guards up. My guard was up because my upbringing taught me that when I opened and showed my true self, people I loved and trusted would mock or tease me. My upbringing taught me that my ideas only mattered if those ideas were in line with my current authority. Deviation from authority was not accepted in the society I was raised in and there was plenty of authority in my upbringing. It included anyone one older than me. This was both a blessing and a suppressant to my self-confidence.

The message I received from those that I knew loved me were messages of encouragement to do, think, and believe as they thought I should. They expected me to pursue their path, walk the journey that they created without any regard of my own passions and desires. My family had no ill regard. With each generation, my family has grown stronger and more successful than the last. They expected me to trust the torch they were proud of and trying to pass to me. But society then, still did not think or expect much by way of education of a Latin girl. My family was living their best prideful selves and did not want me to get hurt.

I took steps in my shoes and fought my first battle within my own family at a very young age. My first memory of doing so was when I was in junior high school. I believe I was in the seventh grade when things I was being taught in my family, just stopped making sense. Before this, I tried to feel the vibes of their ways. But could not. I began visualizing more possibilities then what my family saw. I wanted to go much further in school than just finishing high school. This is where the ripples in the water of my life began.

I felt alone much of the time, but I continued to walk in my shoes. With decades behind me of walking in my shoes, I have finally arrived at a place of love and acceptance. I am proud to say that I do not fit the primeval vision of many of my family members, but many of them now see my vision and they too breathe well in this space. I have finally arrived to love and acceptance. I love my family, as they love me. It has not been easy, but the possibilities of our capabilities are now the focus of what I see around me. We stuck it out together. Our love for each other has always been there, not without resistance, but there, nonetheless. Step into your shoes. Those that truly love you may not be able to feel your journey. Stay brave as you step in your shoes without worries of losing anyone that is important in your life. Important people may not understand the climb of your journey, but important people will not fault and will remain in your life always. Stop and realize that your heart's draw is special.

Here, as I speak to you, I realize that I am special; we all are. You are special. Everyone is special. To one another we may not be special, but to our Creator we are. But not so special that He would ever have us alone. We were not created to be alone. We are not ever alone. When you find yourself feeling down and/or alone, stop, take a deep breathe, and say those words to yourself, "Someone does understand".

Create this moment for yourself, you have time. It will not take much time. This is a simple affirmation you can give to yourself at any moment. Believe and allow your resistance to go. Step into your shoes. Step into your new season and persevere forward. In your shoes, you will stand taller and braver. When your next journey begins, when you reach the next fork in the road. Know there will be forks.

What do I do during these times, when I am between forks in the road and I feel I am just strolling along? I let my guard down, so to speak. Some may call it a waste to not pay close attention to everything, especially having gone through so much in the last crossroad. For me, I find, I must. I need to breathe. You may need to breathe, enjoy, and focus, during certain points of life too. Why not take this breathe during moments when the journey is straight and after a major decision? Especially after meeting a personal milestone.

For example, the many years I devoted all my free time, and then some, to completing my BBA and studying for the CPA license exams. That journey may seem simple for some but was difficult for me. I had a quit my job that I worked at for over eight years in order to attend the university of my choice. Many people I knew shunned me during this time. They proclaimed, some loudly in my ear that, I thought I was better than them. A "Ms. Goody Two Shoes". There were so many serious and heavy decisions that I had to make. The lighter of these decisions included giving up the safeguard of employer-provided health care and my steady income. But, once the decision was made, and I was living and breathing in the new space, there was just no reason or room to think about the decision any more. I worked hard and earned this moment. I found it best to make the most of the choice and enjoy this new season of my life without fear as I walked in my shoes.

Trust the decisions and the choices you make while walking in your true shoes. Your true shoes will take care of you on the journey. Have faith and trust without stress. Breathe and reap the reward of this part of the journey where you work on that specific milestone or goal you have decided on with the worry and pondering behind you, even if you are and/or feeling alone at the moment. Stay focused. Be your best self in all moments, especially in moments where you are readying and resting your mind for the next major decision that will need to be made. We all know, all too well, that there is sure to be a next major decision point ahead. Know that we are lucky that there will be more trails ahead. More woos in life equals more growth in your life. There are bigger and better things that your today self could not even imagine being possible.

The journey I stepped in my shoes, to get my college degree, included resetting a tone for my family. Your journey may differ. But this journey of mine may have similarities to yours. I stepped into my shoes to walk in unchartered and unknown territory for my family and me. I followed my heart and allowed my spirit to hold and guide me. I had hopes for acceptance, even hopes for others to follow, or at least the hopes of paving a path where others could know that there are choices. For me, it was that a college degree is possible for us. That a dream, a vision of a degree and a career is not just for those we work for. I believe that the time and dedication to complete this mile stone is well worth the investment. I am the first in my family to pursue and complete a 4-year degree and any certification, to have worked for prestigious organizations and held respectful titles. I have made strides with no regret, for my hard work and legacy of others I "left" behind; those that abandoned me while I focused on this journey. Some friends and even family believed I abandoned "our ways" or believed that I thought I was better than them. The amount of negativity energy around me during this transitional phase was more than anyone could bear if given a moment to ponder it. So, I stepped in my shoes and did not ponder it.

Stay focused, believe and trust in your journey. Step in your shoes, free of this noise. Step into your shoes and walk your best self, strong, bold, and proud. Your past does not define your future. You are not part of any statistic.

Statistics do not define you
Statistics defines no one

A statistic is an event or person regarded as only a piece of data. Statistics cannot define me. Statistics cannot define you. Statistics define no one. We are all so much more than a piece of data. Key word being "piece" and a piece of anything cannot define any whole being.

I walk strong in my shoes, bold and proud, as you need to, regardless of the countless statistics others may try to believe that you are.

The society I grew up in consisted of many moments that would be considered by many as an opportunity to label me with a statistic. I choose to view my moments as blessings. I have many childhood memories of seeing adults drinking excessively. Females were tools to some and not taken serious even in the work place. These were difficult waters to navigate.

Regardless of the many trials, mixed messages, difficult times, and tragedies that I have witness, I have made it through them and consider myself blessed to live each day.

Choose to find and focus on blessings. Do not focus on the darkness that you witness which can shadow the belief that you hold for your journey. Even if others cannot see your vision. The journey that your shoes call you to step into and walk in belongs to you. It is already yours. All you need to do is step to begin your journey.

The first "statistic" that I carry is being a victim of aggravated sexual assault. I was a young child. That day became, what many would perceive, as a tragic statistic, and for many years I believed the same. Today I choose to recognize that I escaped and survived my attacker. Yes, I have unseen scars. I have a phobia that rises in certain circumstances because these scars that others cannot understand, and I choose not to explain. But I survived the event and continue to survive the scars of the event. I am here and I am alive. I am not a statistic, a piece of data. Instead I am a survivor. It was an unfortunate moment that I experienced, but I am not a statistic because of this experience. What I am is, blessed. Blessed to have been saved from this tragic situation and others I have come across. You too can overcome any and every tragic moment that you may have experienced and survived! You are never a statistic. Do not walk in a journey of labels. Walk your journey and over obstacles with the feeling of the blessing that you made it across.

Growing up, I found comfort in school, in learning, and from classmates that where interested in learning as well. There is power in numbers. Surround yourself with those that are also stepping in their shoes journeying on to their greater place. The community I was blessed with was in a new school. Soon, I found my laughter again and dove into my class work. I worked hard and graduated junior high school with honors, past the high school entrance exam, and earned an invitation for admission to an elite high school that specialized in science, technology, engineering, and mathematics. Look and find the comfort of the journey that your true shoes can and do provide.

Due to another unfortunate incident, I only attended school there for two years. An outsider made his way past security and cornered me in an empty stairway. Nothing happened, I only got scared and reported the incident. My father immediately came to and signed me out of that school and into the local school closer to home. This was my father's way of protecting me. The experience in my next school was so different. There were so many that took pleasure in mocking and teasing others just because of race, social status, or lack thereof. I was so confused and began believing the terrible things that kids and even adults would say. Someone told me that the only reason I could attend a school in this "prestigious" Lower Brooklyn Bay area was because my parents mopped the floors in a building we could never afford to live in. My world began collapsing. I begged and pleaded to get back in my first high school. When that did not work, I protested, complained, and criticized.

I felt everything I had worked so hard on for years was gone and all my accomplishments were diminished to nothing. I was 15 years old and as hard as I tried, I could not find any help. I felt lost and helpless, became depressed, and started cutting classes here and there because I felt defeated completely lost.

Being a short stature girl being raised in a large city, I was taught to smile and say thank you to kitten calls, to watch for predators that befriend their prey, and other survival tactics. I had my fair share of experiences by this age to understand how important these lessons were. Walking to school, going to the store, going anywhere was overwhelming. I felt I was in a war of harsh streets within my own home area.

I did not know what to do with what I was experiencing. I tried to seek help from hotlines and counselors but was not given any other direction than "talk to your parents". There was no talking. I stopped going to school and stayed home instead. My outside world was more than I could manage at this age. So, I decided to just complete my GED when I was old enough to do so, without asking for permission to do so from anyone, and moved on from my dreaded high school experience.

My spiral continued soon after when I found out I was pregnant. I decided I would keep my baby. Where I grew up, girls were safer when they had a child in tow, and I was ready for a new life. The thought of not having my baby was not a thought I ever entertained. I trusted this part of my journey and knew this was a blessing. I was scared but knew I would figure this out. I knew I could finally move on from here, leave the old season behind, and step into my new season shoes.

Just before I was 17 years old, I was a high school drop-out and a teen mom. By 18 years old, I was a mom again. I had my own home when I went into the hospital and homeless by my release three days later. No one came to visit my daughter and I during my hospital stay. My parents were now living out of state, halfway across the country. I remember sitting alone, watching the world go by from the hospital window, wondering where were those that cared about me. Not here, not any more. That night at the hospital was one of the loneliest moments of my life.

There are more statistics I collected before, during, and after all of this. So many more trials that make those I survived through childhood seem like pebbles on the road, but this is enough to speak of for now. Just know, *someone does understand.*

Please stop feeling alone, you are not, no one is. You can rise above anything you are faced with. You can rise above it ALL. You know you are strong. You know you can. Your only fear is the fear of being *alone* in uncharted waters. Just because you cannot see or touch someone does not mean that they are not out there. You are not alone! Not now, not ever!

I speak from someone who feels, at times, they have made it somewhere but nowhere at the same time. I have made it somewhere in accordance to where I come from; but nowhere in comparison to those who are where I am at. It is a confusing place to be.

When you are the one paving new roads, with no one immediately available in your toolbox to help you navigate, you feel you walk in your shoes alone, and, in the dark. This is okay, just walk in your shoes with pride in your heart. Grab hold of and carry belief and do your best. You can only hope that others may follow down the path where you have passed and shed light on, making the possibility known to them. You must believe that the future of your generations to come will be forever changed, even if you feel at times that you are failing to complete the journey. Know that you are setting a path of possibilities beyond what anyone before you has ever done. Take pride in that! Own that pride. That pride is yours! Continue walking in your shoes and carve a new path of possibilities for others after you to walk in. Fear not to walk past what generations before you have taught you. Explore, journey on, and create something, a path, that your generations to come will have no concerns walking on or memory of how it was paved. It can be and is scary, yes, many, many times over. But it is also so worth it. Take pride and walk in your shoes.

Realize that you will make mistakes. Mistakes are a part of the journey. Learn from each one you make and use that learning as you continue. Other families have had a person who was strong, as you are strong. They too made mistakes but not the mistake of quitting, or even worse, not trying. There may be times you will need to slow the progress of your progression and it may seem like it is taking much of a long while, but never give up on it. If it calls to you, continue walking, even if you must take small steps. Continue foraging forward, relentless, and regardless of time.

Time. No, lack thereof, carve out time

I have spent plenty of time looking for time and even discussing how much time I do not have. No time to do this that and/or the other. Sounds a bit of an oxymoron, doesn't it?

One day I was speaking to a co-worker. We bumped into each other while leaving a presentation given by a guest speaker at our company about her new book. This co-worker made a comment about not having time to join a book club, a topic we were discussing. I responded, with little thought, "We all have time, it is just a matter of how we use it.". Saying this out loud, and being comfortable to do so, allowed me to not only hear the words but also acknowledge its meaning. The comfort I felt, I realize, resulted from me stepping into my shoes. To explain, months before this moment, I found myself uncomfortable around this person. We had an uncomfortable moment in a meeting a few months prior, or, at least, it was uncomfortable to me. It started with a comment she made in the meeting, which the content does not matter. What matters is that I placed a protective distance between myself and her ever since that moment. I knew what I was doing but that did not improve the situation. I felt awkward when we would cross paths in the office, and it did not help matters we worked for the same group. The day we left the speaking event, I found myself side by side with her and I was not uncomfortable. What made this encounter different than the countless ones before? The difference was I was feeling inspired and empowered by the speaker at the event and left the event walking in my shoes.

Instead of placing boundaries, it does us a greater justice to walk in our shoes with pride and confidence and a simple well feeling of self. This is a much better place to experience the world and life around us.

Although we have yet to join a book club together, we still share this common interest of reading inspirational books, just about every chance we get. These chance meetings are a quick run in at the office when our paths cross. Even if we only have one or two minutes, two times a month, we stop and speak. The point is, we *find* some time, not much, but some time. Because of this, I am connected to another person and that connection is a positive connection. She even surprised me one day with a "Gratitude-Gram", a token where in the office we can offer and recognize one other for anything positive. It read, "For a mutual lover of books". I was wow stricken and forever humbled by this gesture. She no longer works there and has moved on to other endeavors. Her absence from my work space is without regret on my end because every day since the event day I enjoyed her kinship. I only hope she took my bond with her and carries it always, as I will hers.

We all know, on the surface, that time is a precious commodity. We further know, that we all have a limited amount of this resource and the quantity of how much we hold is unknown. This truth comes to light anytime we hear of someone near death or passing. More so, when you know the person and they are near and dear to you.

I stopped for some time connecting with anyone after the sudden loss of my dearest and closest friend. My sister from another mother, godmother to my son, great and best friend of my mother. She was my family, down to my core. I was so grief stricken that I did not even realize that I was pushing most everyone away from me. I did this at that moment when I withdraw from a great mentor and boss, and for years after. As I write this, this is where I pause. Years! I wrote years, and yes, it has been over five years since I suffered this lost. That is a lot of time spent and gone that I can never recover. This truth saddens me. This sadness creates a crossroad for me. I can continue to walk in sadden shoes or I can step into *my* shoes. I walked in sadden shoes long enough. Spent and invested enough time in them. Those sadden shoes have led me through much emptiness. Upon reflection, I notice time. There is no lack thereof. Rather choices we make moment by moment on how to spend it.

When we say, "I don't have time", or "I wish I had the time to do this, that, or the other", many times, we are not being honest with ourselves. Days, months, and years are made of time. We all have obligations where some or most of our time must be spent, but time encompasses your day, every day, and we all have moments where we spend time frivolously and if not, then maybe you can consider a time swap, if even only for a short while. Swap out something you do today for something you want to try. If it does not fit as you expected, you can always switch back. But when you make a swap, give the new a *real* try.

For years, maybe since I was in the eighth grade, I dreamed of being able to go to school and complete a college degree. The vision I had in my head was so complete. Being from Brooklyn, New York, I envisioned that the school building would be historical in its architecture, beautiful and classical. But when I moved from Brooklyn to Dallas, I was a high school drop-out, not yet 20 years old with two children, and in a marriage that was collapsing, not to mention homeless. I was lucky enough to get a job as a cashier at a large auto parts store. The job was just that, a job and good enough for the moment, but I needed more. I wanted opportunity.

I walked in my shoes, stood on what little experience I had, from my previous wholesale cashier job I held in Brooklyn and soon moved from that job to a full-time job with a check cashing company. There I was nurtured. I was taught about the business and eventually was given a store to manage. During this time, I separated from my husband, became a single mom, and had my own apartment with my kiddos. I was now 20 years old. So much accomplished in a little time but not any real feat, I must admit. Having moved from Brooklyn to Dallas in 1990, the cost of living was nothing in comparison. I did nothing different in Dallas than what I was doing in Brooklyn. The only difference was the Dallas location provided me much more for my efforts and my low pay. Finding the time to work on my dream of completing a college degree while working full time, and mom of two toddlers would prove to be an immense challenge.

My living situation was far from ideal. Our apartment was crawling with roaches. The infestation so bad I could not cook a meal or have any food in the apartment. I would not even go into my own kitchen. The place was down-right nasty!

My daughters and I remained in that apartment for a few months, but I did not feel safe there. I moved in with my boyfriend with my daughters after some talks with him of where I wanted to go next with my life. My boyfriend, later husband, was on board to protect us, provide us with a better place to be, and help me with my next steps. The thought of needing some help from someone I had only known for under a year filled me with anxiety, but I was sure we would all be safer with him than alone in that nasty apartment.

Soon after the move, I completed my GED and my college road began. It was 1992. I graduated with my 4-year degree in December 2005. You do the math. It took me well over 4-years to complete this journey. I did not have the *time* to work full-time, go to school full time and raise 3 children; as I had my third daughter at the end of 1994.

I divorced for the second time in 1996. Even though we are no longer married, he is still family just in a different sense. He is a good man and has a wonderful family. I am blessed to have had their support then and their love now.

Time was most definitely a factor, a wall, but I stayed in my shoes. My determination to become a college grad was strong while I was stepping in my shoes. This journey was mine to step in and own. So, no matter how many times I came across hurdles or stones that kept me from signing up for the next semester, I kept seeking a way to complete this part of my journey. I kept changing where I focused my very little downtime.

Those shoes where one of the toughest that I have worn in my life; the shoes that took me through my journey through college graduation, that is. Finding the time to stay true to my shoes to complete this journey, that I was so determined to fulfill, was painful, in many ways, many times over. I had to tell family members, love ones, "No, I can't" on so many occasions, I may have sounded like a broken record. Most of those closest to me could not figure out what the heck I was doing. When you grow up in a family where you are the first to journey through college, at times, there is just no explaining your "why".

One of the mottos in the society I grew up in was, "children should be seen and not heard". Then, when you become an adult, you get a sense of freedom from the bullshit that was once placed on you. This can cause some misguidance which can direct you to believe that 'your time' has arrived and it is time to enjoy life and have 'fun'. Misguidance can include forgetting the authority of school or to have no worries about the bills today. Fun is all that matters. Just have fun today and you can figure out tomorrow, tomorrow. But tomorrow never seems to come. Many live for today and do not worry about tomorrow. I had much of this around me.

I saw so much time spent on nothing and everyone around me was the same. I did not fit in with this way of living, not when I was stepping in my shoes, anyhow.

One by one and moment by moment, even if only five minutes here and there, I began rallying up my time by stopping any of my actions that did not pay dividends towards my tomorrow. It was one day and one small choice at a time. I even cut off people that gobbled up my time talking nothing more than nonsense, drama, and began seeking like mind thinkers to draw strength from. No, I did not believe that I was better than anyone. I was just changing my focus and holding myself true to my shoes. If I wanted something different in my life, I needed to spend my time differently. I needed a change. If someone did not love and respect me for doing so, they did not love and respect me. Simple! Difficult? Yes, but simple.

Change is never easy. This decision, this change, sometimes left me feeling lonely and disconnected to the only self that I was familiar with, but a self I could not make sense of. A world that I questioned, time and time again.

I find as we age, great friends that you can connect become increasingly difficult to make. Staying true to my shoes, I needed, for myself, to solve this problem I was having. So, I joined a book club. Here I could meet people in a safe environment where there is a common thread, the book we are all reading at the same time. The book club meets just one hour a month to discuss a pre-selected book. I felt, and still do, that I have no time to read. So instead, I get the audio version of the book and listen to it in the car during my daily commute. I swapped my commute time of listening to music and news to listening to the book. The transition was difficult at first, as I would zone and tune the book out, but soon I got used to it. Today my commute needs an audio book and my connection with my book club is priceless to me. I have not found my next great friend yet, but I do enjoy this great group and it gives me something positive to aim towards as well as a sense of community. A small, yet significate, connection.

If you want change, if you need a change, take inventory on how you spend your time. When I started a weight loss program. I realized that I needed to document and understand what my eating habits where. I spent a month making no change other than downloading a nutrition app and documenting everything I would eat, with absolute honesty. At the end of the month, I reviewed my results and started making small changes to my daily choices. This conscience awareness and small changes led to me losing weight and keeping it off. I apply the same to how I spend my time. Take inventory of your time. Start with small changes if you need to but start today. Make choices that invest in your better tomorrow and do not lose sight of even the smallest connections.

Make Connections – even the smallest matter

Most of us can agree that connecting with others is important to our being. It is a part of our fabric and our essence. There are far too many times we focus on deep, large, or, what we perceive as, an important connection. I know have done this in my life. But the fact is that all connections serve a purpose. Be it small, medium, or large. For a season of your life, years, months, days, or even minutes. Perceived importance has nothing to do with impression or impact. If they are positive, they *all* matter just the same.

When I first moved over 1,500 miles from my hometown to start a new life in a part of the country where no one I knew was familiar with, those I was closest to either thought I was crazy, believed I would come back, or felt that "you can take the girl out of Brooklyn but you can never take Brooklyn out of the girl". Well, only one was correct. Brooklyn has never left this girl. Part of what we are is a product of our upbringing and one cannot remove or replace who they are at their core. I am here to tell you that the transition, even almost thirty years later, has never been easy and is still not complete. I recognize that I continue to mature in my journey, always.

Being born in Brooklyn, New York in 1971 and moving to Dallas, Texas in 1990 was an extreme culture clash. I was a high school dropout with two children and in a marriage that was collapsing. In Brooklyn, I had my friends, great friends for that season in my life. These friends understood me and encouraged me. We were so close, and no one knew me better or believed in me more than they did. I had extended family in New York, who, though supportive and loving, could not seem to understand me or my journey. In Dallas, I had my immediate family, my mom, dad, and grade school baby sister. These were folks that always struggled to understand my true core but loved me, by a lack of anything better than default. It was difficult for me to be without my close group of friends, the circle in which I have never felt more at home with, to move to a place I was unfamiliar with.

It aches me to admit the truth about my decision to move. I made the move because I could no longer survive in Brooklyn. I was homeless, sleeping from home to home and a couple of times in unlocked cars on snowy days with my toddler daughter in tow and a newborn housed somewhere safe. I had to do something different.

Settling into Dallas left me feeling empty and alone, even though I had my mom and a dad in Dallas who loved me. Still, in my soul, they were not like my close group of friends, the ones who knew and understood me. My friends were people who I could confide anything and everything to with little explanation. Rather, I would receive guidance that was always positive, true, and hard core. You had to be a part of to understand and appreciate. The closeness of that group of friends is now long gone. They are too far and unfamiliar with my new life, as I am theirs, to offer the strength and support that I once drew from them.

My move to Dallas was before Facebook and cellphones. Making and keeping connections before this technology commanded more time, money, and presence. But I never stopped trying to connect with others in that special way. I even made a few more very close friends who will remain forever in my heart. Unfortunately, these friendships were made at work. Because I had small children, work was where I spent just about every waking social moment I had available. Since our common thread was work, once we moved to other companies, so did the time we would spend together and the knowing of one another thins. The convenience of our meet ups was gone when jobs changed, and since we never went out of our way to see each other before, why would we start now? After the work separation? I tried to connect live a few times and my heart knows we are still friends. I know we have a sense of love for one another. Unfortunately, it seems only on Facebook though, as with my hometown close group of friends. When convenience is removed and replaced with distance, along with an old subject matter replaced with a new job, a new company, new people, and the separation continues to grow, soon the friendship becomes a faded beloved memory, or a convenient touch point received only by a scroll down a Facebook page or a personal post to say "Happy Birthday" once a year. To any of my girls that are reading this, they know who they are, I know that they feel the same mist that has moved over our past connection. But I also know that they feel my love, just as I feel theirs. I am forever grateful to hold their love because I know they hold mine. All connections matter.

I am out of touch with so many relationships with people I was once so very close to at some pivotal point in my life, regardless of the love I know we hold for each other. As I think about the importance of connections, even giving a minute of negative thoughts to this is too long. I have thought our friendship was not as important to them as it was to me. This taught was because, when I would reach out and invite for meet ups, I received so many, "I cannot", or got stood up last minute. Giving this too much thought led me to believe that they no longer considered me as a today friend, and maybe that is true. But they remain, and always will be, a friend of my heart, forever. This juncture is just a transition of a season. They are today, and will always be, important to me and will always be welcomed in my life, any time. We will just pick up where we left off. The love I hold for them is that accessible to me and this is a more amazing way for me to hold on to these connections.

If you feel your true friends no longer feel close to you, you might be entering a change of season in your life. If this is so, you may begin to see some friends as shoestring friendships. Take care because if you do not recognize that the new space between these friends results from a new season of your life beginning, which is a beautiful opportunity to grow, you may place resentment on people that have had an important impact on your life. Some people that where involved within a particular season of your life are true connections that cannot be broken. Connections matter, even when the "how" of the friendship changes. Failing to recognize the true connections you make in a season of your life can lead you down a depressive road. Instead, reach for the love you know was, is there, and will always be there. Even if it is not as close as it was before. The importance can still be tangible. Take the love, blessings, and all you have learned with you forward as seasons change. All connections matter.

When I realized that I was not recognizing a pivotal changing point in my life, I also realized that I was preventing myself from seeing new connections that surrounded me daily. The longing I had to remain in a prior season of my life, the life I had grown accustom to, was preventing me from living and engaging in my current life. I was missing my newly erected season. When I stepped into my shoes and began to pay attention to my today, I found, I was surrounded by many people that like me for me. I was placing resistance against making theses connections and keeping these new connections from forming. I was not walking in the right shoes to meet up with the new connections that surrounded me.

So, a change was needed. With no thought of a cause or fault, I stepped into my shoes and make a conscience effort not to wear and walk in the shoes that were part of my past season. Wearing old season shoes is like trying to move a large rock instead stepping on and over it. Chasing the wonderful moments of my past were bumming me out often, not to mention, placing a shadow on my present day. By changing and walking in my today shoes, I have come across a connection that is larger than large. It is huge. A person who is so much like me, she might as well be me. Along the way in my shoes, my current shoes, I continue to make small and medium connections. One or two seem to be developing into large. It is all coming together for me again and it feels amazing.

Step into your shoes and understand that associates are associates, friends are friends, and sometimes distance can move friends from beloved friends to associates, even true friends can turn into associates. Seasons change. It is just that and nothing more. It is not less love. My past connections are as important to me as my current connections, but the past cannot be forced to be kept the same light in our future. Always a part of us just, sometimes, not in the same light. Step into your shoes. Do not disregard new connections that can turn into friendships because you revert to keeping an awesome past alive in your current situation. Not that you should not hold people from your past special in your heart. Afterall, they are part of makes you, you. And you are great. Every part that makes you, you is great and important. Remain present in your life and notice when a season ends and a new one is blooming.

I, admittingly, still find myself, feeling lonely and desiring a reconnection someday, that old familiar feeling creeping back up on me. When this happens, I know what shoes to wear. I put them on and accept the smallest connections I am blessed with daily. A smile from a child while shopping in a store, for example. I receive the blessing. Even a stranger I walk pass in my office. I work in a large office complex. The one thing I do every day is smile and 99% of the time I receive a smile in return. Smiles are free, fabulous, and infectious. I have connected with people that I would not have otherwise meet all because of the smiles I give while walking in my shoes. I take comfort that I may have made a difference in someone's day. They might have been having a bad day but not for that moment. The moment they receive my smile.

Step into your shoes and make every day better for yourself and perhaps for others as well. Each and every single day, they all matter.

Make Each Day Better
They _ALL_ matter

For many years, I have always wanted to write a book, not that I imagined that anyone would ever want to read it, but just something I was driven to accomplish. I have very little training in writing, only the basic English classes I took my freshman year in college. I do not know what could have possessed me to want to write a book. Afterall, I am an accountant, for crying out loud, not a writer. But I am a firm believer that, if a possibility enters your heart, then your mind, body, and spirit can accomplish it. You just need to power through trial and error, and you will learn what it takes to get it done.

I have started and stopped over a dozen attempts on writing a book in my pursuit to accomplish this possibility of mine. All of which centered on the same story. Before I would begin my next attempt, I would read books to teach myself how to write a novel, believing that a novel would be the best way to tell my story. I would start and stop writing. I have even reached out to mentors and a ghostwriter. Nothing seemed to help to keep me engaged. I was crushing myself with every stop. It is so frustrating when your heart desires something and your mind refuses to deliver it. Why couldn't I do what I wanted so much to do?

Instead of getting angry and allowing frustration to get the best of me, I would walk away from that current attempt. Walking away during these moments made my days to follow better. Rather than spending time dealing with personal frustrations of what I could have perceived as a short coming in my lack of writing skills, I stepped away and continue to enjoy my family and my present life. I stepped away in my shoes which allowed me to stay centered in my life. I realized the book, that I had yet to write was not happening because of two things; Timing and Approach.

I travel in my shoes with a daily focus of counting my blessings and smiling, every day. There were days that I had to dig deep to find my focus, but I always find a reason to smile. These better day shoes have led me to both the right time and the right approach, this book here. My journey to share my story with you did not come without frustrations and an immense share of sinking feelings. Though once there, at the place that my shoes where taking me to, the words flowed so well that sometimes my pen could not keep up with my thoughts. I reached the place where I was called to be and only because I trusted in my shoes. A trust that took me decades to build, only due to my silliness. All I needed to do was stop trying to control everything, stop listening to the fear engrained in me from childhood. Rather, I placed trust in myself and the shoes I knew were mine and walked in them with trust and confidence.

It was during this writing, the writing of this book, that I began reflecting. What made this time so different from the dozens of times before? My shoes changed, and nothing more.

Months before, after my last two failed book writing attempts, which were well thought out and structured, so I thought, I flipped my focus on spending what little free time I could muenster up, doing me. Doing me, unapologetically, with no expectations, no excuses, no framework, no guide, and no outline. Doing just me, working on being the best me I can be. Just taking my steps, in my shoes. I broke down and prayed to God. I threw to Him what I could not handle in my life, all that I could no longer carry at the moment. Relieving myself from the mental stress of all that I was carrying. I gave control up to God and stayed walking in my shoes to see where they, He, would take me.

I began firmly believing I am worth scheduling time in my own life for. You too are worth your own time! Not an easy thing to do. Yes, I understand! As a mother of four who works a career full time, supports a business and has three grandchildren, believe you me, I know, there is no time for "me". I say, stop working to find this "me" time, just step in your shoes and if your heart truly desires something, doing what you do and staying true to you, your shoes will lead you towards small pieces of fulfillment. Keep your eyes open because serenity moments are indeed on your path. Stop and pick up those jewels that await you on your path. Small or large, they all matter. Take in a breath, enjoy the jewels and your breath as well. Even if it is just a sunrise or sunset you happened to witness, acknowledge those moments in your day. Let go of frustrations and any such thoughts; instead, enjoy every moment of your journey and begin incorporating you back in your journey.

Explore Incorporating "You" Back in Your Life

One day, as I clicked along the web, something which seems we all spend some time doing, I came across a ½ day class to learn about taking photos using studio lighting. Photography has always been a special interest of mine, a hobby I enjoy fine tuning. I never felt inspired to make a livable wage doing this full time, as others have and do, but I do love learning more and more about it.

Before coming across this class, I recall having a heart to heart with my husband. The topic was how I wished we could, actually, how I wished *he* would spend more time with me. I was telling him how I was feeling lonely. Truth is, I was seeking him to problem solve for me, hoping he would offer me the solution to solve my loneliness. He told me I should get out more, get involved, and find people of my similar interests. At the moment, I took this as rejection, because at the moment, I was feeling down. "Why didn't he offer to do something with me that would help me feel better?", I thought to myself, rather than offer me an avenue to seek companionship elsewhere?

Wow! I felt, for lack of a better term, like a pain in his ass. My translation, which I own, was, "Go get something else going on and leave me alone". Don't get me wrong, he did not intend to come across this way at all. I love my husband and he did mean well, but at that moment, I took his comment negatively. But I have learned that I must own my love for this man, and when something like this conversation creates a statement, that I may not like on the surface, I work on owning my feelings. Sometimes, not fast enough, I admit. I think as myself as a constant work in progress. I smile here.

It serves us best to step back, pull back, and stop those comeback comments for rushing off the tongue. Sometimes it is best to continue a dialogue later when we are in a better place to reflect and receive the remark as it was meant by the giver. This is not to give kudos to him, but instead, to realize that I trust this man enough to be my husband for all these years and I must be able to entertain the comments from those I trust and love, even if, when given, I am not able to receive it well. I must take the message and revisit later, when I can and am able to receive it.

OMG, this can be beyond difficult. It can be and is extremely hard, but only at that moment! Especially since we now live in an era of immediate gratification. We must relearn, or learn for the first time, that not all suitable informational input is going to be delivered to us immediately. Things that are most important to come to us when we are ready to receive. We must realize that, at times, we are not ready to receive important feedback immediately. This is where lessons from yoga help – child's pose.

So, along with signing up for the photo class, I had also saved for and scheduled for a personal trainer three times a week. I try being a bit of a physical fitness "nut", on and off. This time found myself with 15 pounds I needed to shed. I also take part in a book club at my local library. Reflection. I revisited the "nerd" within myself. I brought this self-nerd back up to my surface. By doing so, I felt myself walking in my shoes again. I spent a brief moment wondering why I neglected this "me" that was always there, and realized, I let myself get so busy in my life, that I slowly, one by one, took pieces of myself and place the pieces on a shelf. I began ignoring those pieces, to the point, that I found myself, within myself, unrecognizable. Motherhood and adulthood have a tendency to do that, to you, if you are not paying attention to you. There is so much you *need* to do *all* the time. I do not say this to encourage anyone to ignore the things that you must accomplish in your day to day, just do not lose and ignore yourself in your journey. Stay in your shoes and if you have stepped out, do not be afraid to explore and walk "you", every now and again, once again. Explore, incorporating "you" back into your life. Small steps, here and there. All steps matter.

Before I hired a personal trainer, I took inventory of my spending habits to see where I could trim back in order to work in this new expense. I started first by cutting personal expenses that were, simply, not offering me anymore than superficial, quick, and small "happiness". There were reckless spending habits I had on a weekly basis that did nothing for my long-term happiness. Daily gourmet coffees included. I changed my habits, and instead, I started saving, both my time and money. I had no idea, at the time, what

I was saving for with the exception that I knew that I was saving for a better me, a change. I did not realize it then, but that was the beginning of this me, stepping back into my shoes. There were months of baby steps, some of which I felt I had no direction. But no matter, I placed trust in my shoes and my confidence increased. Confidence, faith, and trust are important at this stage. During these times, months and months of time, I made it a point to do one small thing that made me feel good in my soul. Even if it was just, simply giving that free smile away or making it a point to look up at the clouds. Something, every day, no matter how small, is something.

Sometimes, things you do for you are large, but these are usually well planned and researched. For example, when I hired that personal trainer for three months. On the other side, some things are small. All are significant.

Make every one of your days better than it would have been if you went through it effortlessly. Even the hard days, where it seems impossible to find anything to uplift you... Step into your shoes, set a timer, if you must, for just three to five minutes, sit down, close your eyes and connect with your breathing. Take a Zen moment. Feel and listen to the breath of you. You are alive and that is a beautiful thing. Make a plan to do so.

Map out your plan

Where are your shoes trying to lead you? How do you get from where you are, to where you belong? When you are looking to achieve a goal, it is important to think of the steps you need to take to get from where you are to where you wish to be. Map out these steps. Begin creating a plan that you can accomplish.

Many folks may be familiar with the "Dave Ramsey Plan". A plan that has helped many to journey to a debt free life. I am sure, those that set out to achieve financial freedom, felt it would not be possible, but knew, they were ready for a change. Ready for controllership of their finances, so gave this plan a whirl, and achieved it. I am sure because this is how my husband and I felt when we came across the Dave Ramsey Plan and set it into action.

My husband and I, like many others, were moving forward in life's financial journey with the aid of lenders, credit, and, of course, debt. Only to, one day, finding ourselves writing checks out each time we got paid and working for the bills we k new were coming. Sometimes we would send out our last dollar, but we paid the bills. We would work, to make money, to pay money we owed. Then we worked more, to make more, to pay more. It was a vicious cycle. Most times we made enough to pay what we owed, except for the most important one of all, ourselves.

Yes! Start a savings plan and pay yourself first!

We read the books, listened to Dave Ramsey's radio program, drank the "Kool-Aid" and got on board. A few years later, it happened. We were debt free. WOW! It forever changed our life and our mindset. It was and is fantastic to be in control and not write our income away every time we get paid. If you are not familiar with this program and are haggling over payments for a house, car, credit cards, furniture, etc… I encourage you to read one or several of his books. Your shoes do not wish you to be in debt. Your shoes wish you freedom from it. Your shoes want to work for you, with you, and not on making payments for materials.

Along those lines, do the same with your personal journey. My first job was as a cashier at an innovative supermarket that was way ahead of its time. It was 1986, and they invested in scanners at the registers that ran on a program of everything in the store based on the item's bar code. Something we all take for granted today. But then, these times, cashiers were still manually punching numbers for the cost of each product that floor people stamped on every single item in the store. Sadly, the market was a short-lived success. But the few months that I was there, I caught on and moved from cashier to head programmer. Though, I made no extra money; I was only 15 years old and the world of computer innovation was being introduced and standing at a register all day was a bore for my shoes. I did not understand it then, but now I realize, that, my shoes where showing me the possibilities of my capabilities.

Seek the possibilities of your capabilities

Years have passed since that first cashier job, but all the while, I still cannot help to continue seeking possibilities of my capabilities. There have been many obstacles I have faced. Most, if not all, I brought on myself via poor decisions made by my immature self. But my inner self, my shoes pulled me always in such a way that I could not ignore. There was something better, and I needed to continue to seek how to make it possible. Regardless of the many statistics I collected against myself along the way.

The statistics I collected were not all by personal choice. Many were by chance, and most all hold a negative connotation. Remember when I said that "someone does understand". Well, I am here to tell you… Forget the statistics, forget data that attempts to label you. Step into your shoes. Every step, every experience, every-day matters in a strong and positive way. Never negative. Steps in your shoes have no tie to negativity. Learn from everything. The good, the bad, and yes, even the ugly.

It was just my journey. Nothing more. Nothing less. There is no sorrow and I hold no shame, at least not any more, as I hold an understanding of the steps I take in my shoes. I am proud to be a licensed CPA who has always and still works hard. I have been blessed with opportunities, knowing that the opportunities were there because I stood and walked proud in my shoes. Strong and firm. The world will know me for me and not my background, my circumstances, or the puddle of mess I was born and raised in, but from those that I rose above.

Never, ever, is it ever too late to step into your shoes. Claim your shoes and begin following what your heart desires, regardless of the noise surrounding you. Did you not excel in school? Did you come from a tough neighborhood or unsupportive family? Have a baby at an early age? Not finish high school and did not go to prom? Do you work your ass off, do a good job, receive excellent performance evaluations but do not get promoted? Yeah, well, that was and, sometimes today, is still me. Are you afraid because you cannot see the "how can I"?

Stop! Stop and silence your negative side and start believing in what is in your heart. Your deeply rooted belief of your capabilities is correct. Step into your shoes and walk your journey. Believe it or not, that path is already there. The path is already yours. You already, and have always, owned your path.

Have faith. Trust and love yourself enough to believe that your dreams are not dreams, but rather are possibilities of your capabilities. You only need to declutter and organize.

Declutter and Organize Mind and Soul, & yes – your space as well

The first two-and-a-half decades of my life was filled with many personal challenges. One of the toughest was mourning the death of two close cousins, who I was very close to. They died too young and just months a part. Someone murdered the first, and the second died after a tragic car accident on his father's, my uncle's birthday. I also mourned close kinships that were living, that I lost to drugs. Before I was twenty-four, I was briefly homeless for the second time in my life, when I left my second, very much loved, husband. The crosses I bared were heavy and some even ugly, but darn it, I was still here. I survived, and my journey continued. Stepping into my shoes, I realized, this was my most important fact to remain focused on.

No step is too small so long as it is in the right direction. Do not waste time wishing your journey to be different, wondering why your now does not look like the one you admire others already have. Want that better paying job? Better credit? Better car? Better life? Look into what it will take to achieve it, then declutter and organize your life to line up with what you wish to achieve. Clean up your path, put your shoes on and begin stepping. Organize the list of tasks that must be completed. Seek to achieve these tasks from easiest to the most difficult. Begin working on things that are immediately possible. When you reach a more difficult task, think of how you can break it down to more manageable subcomponents. For example, if you have a desire to compete a four-year degree on your list. Break that down. What degree do you wish to pursue? What classes are needed to obtain this degree? Research, visit a campus, talk to a college counselor. The cost to do this is only time, no money. Once you understand the classes need, list the classes separately. The last thing you should concern yourself at this stage is the cost. If, because of time and money, you cannot take the recommended 4–5 classes per semester, break that down further. Can you take two classes? If not, most can make room for one class. Chip away at it and eventually you will get there, so long as you work at it, you will complete this milestone too. I promise you that no one will ask you how long it took you to achieve your goal. All that will matter is that you accomplished it, and once you do, no one can ever take it away from you.

I had this dream, and it felt so impossible when I looked at the long list and time commitment. Nonetheless, I jumped in and began my journey in 1992. I graduated with my bachelor's degree in Business Administration (BBA) with a concentration in Accounting in December 2005. You do the math of how long it took me to complete this four-year degree plan. There were semesters that I was not able to take a class for this or that reason. But no worries because credit for classes taken do not expire quickly and can be carried forward. Even if there was a class or two that I took early on that I was at risk of losing to expiration, no whip! I just took the class again at the end during my senior year. It turned out to be a welcomed break to take an "easy" class then. A freshman level class during senior year?

Yes! It felt like a much-welcomed break and not like additional work or effort. After all the difficult classes I had been through, my more mature self was happy to take two "easier" classes during my final semester, one of which was a gym like class. And guess what…??… I DID IT! I graduated! And guess what. No one has ever asked me, at any job interview, how long did it take me to complete my degree. Nope. They only care that I have the degree if the job required it. I did it and so can you! This or any large dream you hold. Good for you for having dreams that seek the possibilities of your capabilities.

Many dreams you may have may seem as if the journey is too difficult, too impossible, riddled with too many obstacles. Sometimes you might venture out and begin your journey, face these real obstacles and begin to second guess yourself. I am here to tell you, if you dream it, all you need to do is believe it, and it is yours to work at and achieve it. You can do it. You can accomplish all that is in your heart to achieve. How do I know? Well, I have never been one to do anything easy. It is just not my style. So, you are probably feeling another story coming on. Yes, you are correct. Here it is.

I was pregnant my final semester of my BBA journey. One morning, about midway through my final semester, I went into labor that could not be stopped and my baby was born over seven weeks premature and was sent directly to the NICU. I share this story with you because you need not worry today about what hurtle you may encounter later at any point along the way. Things that you are working hard on and are focused on have a way of working out, even with challenges met. Even given this challenge, I was able to complete all my classes thanks to a wonderful faculty, great classmates, amazing family, and a delightful hospital staff. I completed all the BBA requirements and qualified for graduation. On the day of my graduation ceremony, I was challenged once again in such a grave way. This challenge had me question if I had chosen the right path and also left me wondering if I should continue the pursuit of this career dream of mine.

On my graduation day, I received a call from a friend who did not call to congratulate me but to deliver a grave message to me instead. Our mutual friend's son, who was in elementary school, was hit by a car on his way home from school. First responders flew him to the local children's hospital by care flight. She called to inform me that our friend was at the hospital, by his side. He was pronounced brain dead on arrival. There was nothing that the medical staff could do for him besides making everyone comfortable as they prepared arrangements for his organ donation.

I have known this friend since before the birth of this child. We worked together, and, for years, we lived in the same town. I had cared for this boy and his brother a few times. Our weekly, monthly, and important life moments included one and other. I love my friend. She and her family were and are my family. There was nothing that could be done but say "Goodbye" to our beloved boy. On my way to my graduation ceremony, my husband and I stopped at the hospital to do just that, say goodbye to this sweet boy. I hugged my friend and said to her, the only thing that could be said, "I love you". She wept in my embrace. This brave woman took notice of me and asked me why I was all dressed up in a business suit, not my normal attire. I somberly reminded her of my graduation. "Oh my God! That's right! Why are you here? Go. Go!", she said to me. I thought, "what a great friend and beautiful person she is". I cherish her so, today and always, even though today distance keeps us from frequent visits we once enjoyed. I embraced her again and left shortly after to head to my graduation ceremony.

My graduation ceremony was so surreal. I was not able to take much of it in and can only recall small bits and pieces of it from my memory. I was so overwhelmed by the day and the moment, not to mention I was lactating terribly. My son was not even two months old yet. The entire day was a magical dream and a horrific nightmare at the same time. It felt like a complete out-of-body experience. It was enough to make even the toughest person pause. Which I did, for days.

I share this story with you to let you know that someone does understand and to never presume that someone else's story is a textbook fantasy, something we are all guilty of envisioning from time to time. Yes, I graduated from a wonderful, private university and completed my four-year degree. Although my journey has been and still is rewarding, my journey to graduation and the day itself was far from it. I survived my tragic graduation day. Still, I cannot and am unable to let go of the pain of a dear friend's loss of her child. So, instead, I carry his memory with pride. I honor the memory of that day for myself, for my friend, for that sweet boy, and for my family. I cannot change what happened, but it would be worse, more tragic, for all, if I did not remain in my journey and continue to walk in my shoes.

Regardless of what you have been up against, you are reading this, which means you are still here. If you cannot let go of an experience, find a way to carry the experience with pride. Experiences are personal building blocks. Those that cannot be forgotten are too far embedded on what makes you, you. Be proud of you. Declutter and organize. Start small if you feel overwhelmed but start. Declutter your living space. What can you clean, put up, donate, give away, and organize and create a visual space and a positive vibe around you? Place things that are in your life in their proper place and stop beating yourself for things that you cannot change or control. Step into a healthier relationship with yourself.

Step out of the abusive relationship you may have with yourself

Working hard and being hard on yourself is a double-edged sword. It can be a motivator and a deterrent at the same time. Begin working on clueing in on these differences. While it is important to tighten up those laces on your shoes and walk in your journey, it is equally important to understand and know when a break is needed and when a break is well deserved.

Know when it is time to rest and recognize when rest time is over. Never spin your wheels. If you find yourself spinning your wheels, stop and reassess your position. Are you tired? What do you need to get back on track? There are 24 hours in a day. In a day, we know that we should sleep for eight of those hours. So, simple math tells us that about 33% of a day should be devoted to sleep. Your mind, body, and spirit need this time to recover from the day and rejuvenate for the next. This leaves 67% of a day to devote on productivity. With 365 days in a year; this means we have about 5,869 hours in a year in which to be productive. Every year.

In case you have not noticed, I enjoy a bit a math here and there.

If you work a full-time job, without overtime, that is 2,080 hours per year dedicated to work. Make those hours count. Do a good job at work. Since you are going to be there anyway, regardless of how you feel about that job, you owe it to yourself, to make that time, your time, count! Learn and do your tasks to the best of your abilities. This leaves you with 3,789 hours remaining in a year. Now, we all know there are other factors to consider, possible overtime, commuting to and from work. So, let us simply round this up and say that you devote 2,800 hours to work. Of course, this is a generalization and is not everyone's reality. Trust me, I understand! My longest work week consumed well over 80 hours in a week. In my profession this is lovingly called "Busy Season". I do not say that to be malice. On the country, I truly enjoyed this part of my career. Done right, a company can make this kind of commitment enjoyable and some work organizations do accommodate this commitment well.

Anyhow, devoting 2,800 hours a year to work would still leave you with 3,069 hours per year, which is just over 255 hours every month. Next, you give some real-life priorities that time. We all have a family, home, faith, friends, and self-relaxation needs. So, getting back to our percentages, except we will round up. Let us say 70% of your time will be spent on your personal priorities. Well, that still leaves you with about 55 hours, each and every month. Call this your spare change. Because it is important to understand that time is just like money. If you do not make a plan for it, your time will spend itself somewhere, without regard for you. Both your time and your money need your direction in order to work for you. Else, it will spend itself without regard for you. So how do you maximize this opportunity of your spare change?

Still do not think like you have any spare time? Oh boy! I was the same. I am a mother of four children, working a full-time job, and have family that always counts on me for things I could not expect or plan for! I hear you! What did I do to make more room? Kaizen! Look at what you do each and every week. How can you make your tasks better so that it takes you less time without costing more money?

I would beat myself silly and tire my mind with the countless chores that I had to accomplish all week long. Of course, all the things I was thinking about had to get done. My family needed to eat, so dinner everyday was on my mind. This was the same with clean clothes, clean house, homework help, etc. Daily. Everyday, all week long, there was something and many times just thinking of it all caused me grave amounts of stress. I was beating myself up, every day, all week long. I needed to find a way to stop this abuse I was inflicting on myself.

For me, one thing, was cooking. I used to cook dinner each night. Rushing home to prep, cook, serve, and clean up after dinner was a daily task that was not always rewarding. So, I found a way to change my approach to this task. Today, I spend one of my days off planning, shopping, and cooking for the entire week. I found I only need to cook about three meals, the rest of the week we could do leftovers, which we did anyway. The planning, shopping, and cooking, which included lunches for the week, only takes me three hours now that I have my select of "go-to meals", which I spend one day on. Dishes, pots, and kitchen are dirty only this one time, this one day, and only for a few hours. I no longer need to clean the kitchen every night, after cooking every evening. We no longer spend time on discussing and debating the night's dinner. Instead, we all get to choose from a pre-set weekly menu. I ask what they would like from the family's weekly menu. It gets pulled out of the refrigerator, plated, heated, and we sit. Dinner is served each evening under 15-minutes. And because everything is planned and pre-done for the week, including our lunches, we eat healthier meals, spend much less money, and waste is kept at a minimal.

To be honest, this was not an easy routine for me to get into. It took many months to get in this routine, and there are times that I do deviate from this routine even still today but when I do, I quickly self-correct and fall back in. The extra work of having to cook and clean up after a meal every day is a quick reminder for me to fall back in preparing meals. It may seem like a crazy way to spend a day off, cooking at least three meals and weekly lunches, but the end result of having piece all week long is sure bliss and works well for us. The dishes that are dirtied daily are nothing that the dishwasher cannot handle. My children play, as does this mom, every evening. I love the harmony this routine brings to my week/workdays. I may spend three hours of my day off to plan and create the meals, but I recover many more hours throughout my week and after a days work and the stress of commuting, I am rewarded with me time on work days. My spare change that I get to spend on me.

I also began washing clothes the last night before the last work week day. For example, if you are off on Saturday and Sunday, then that would be Thursday. Why? Because who wants to do laundry on the weekend? And staying up a little late to complete this task at the end of the work week, well, by this point I am tired anyway, but tomorrow is my FRIDAY! This is motivation enough. Have children? Get the kiddos involved too, regardless of age! Make it a thing. Show them. Do this together. If you live within a family unit, everyone has dirty clothes, so why not wash them together? When you think about it, there are HUGE breaks in between. If you set a day and all know the day, then the one day should not be a problem. This is a great way to show children responsibilities and can even provide an opportunity to connect with them further.

Take 100% full responsibility

I have more honesty for you. I have been married three times, divorced two times as I write this. I have four children, two from my first marriage and one from each of my proceeding marriages. It has taken me all this time, until this moment, to fully conceptualize that I am 100% responsible for all my success as well as my failures, past and future. Sure, I am not to blame for the actions of others, but I am to blame for not recognizing myself, my shoes, and my journey when I set foot on these paths. At the moment, they all seemed as the correct path to take and, perhaps, at the moment they were. Maybe out of some necessity, but my marriages did not "fail" solely because of the other that was involved. Instead, they failed, in part, due to me. Here is where I take 100% responsibility.

When I truly think about it, I have always known who I am and where I belong at my core and my two failed marriages happened, partly, because I was simply not honest with myself or carried fear onto my journey. I was acting simply, I thought, to survive. Then once I got beyond survival and the relationship no longer fit and I was ready to continue, then, "that" relationship no longer worked. Those are the simpler relationships to break free from but do leave casualties to tend to for a lifetime.

Please, please, please, do not get me wrong, each one of my children are my jewels. Even after decades, I firmly believe, each one of my children would tell you, should you ask, regardless of any and all the heartaches, we are in it together. I am here and take 100% full responsibility for any and all the negativity my choices may have caused them and myself. I could have, somehow, chosen a different path. But I did not. So today, and always, I accept 100% responsibility.

With this acceptance, along the realization that my children have endured challenges because of my choices, has brought me some mental peace that lead me to a better place to be a better me, and better mom. Stop worrying about where another person blames should be, as this only deters where your responsibilities lie. Let others worry about themselves and if you cannot trust that, then let the universe worry about them. Worry about you and the universe will take care of them.

I made mature decisions while at an immature stage in my life. I take that with me forward. Even at the start of my current marriage, I think perhaps I was not clear within myself, and maybe I did more than what I was comfortable with because that is what I do. Though, this leaves me feeling like I have to carry much more than I can bare. But that is no one's error, only my own. I take 100% responsibility, finally, for that. I am only happy to have finally discovered it before my demise or the demise of yet another marriage, but where does this leave me today?

I was not sure that I could rebuild a relationship to one I so desire to be in long term. Where, through my actions, I had created something other than. I take 100% full responsibility that I cannot fault someone else's steps to see my own, when I spent so much time in a strengthen journey that I simply did not have the long-term capability to withstand. I realized that, for the most part, I am weaker than I let on. I need to find a way to stop my own madness against myself. To somehow find a way to trust that others will keep me loved, as how I see love is. Trouble is, what does love look like when I am not the one carrying the torch?

I will trust and walk in my shoes. This trust, this walk brought me to a place to a peaceful place in my current marriage and I am proud to say we are seventeen years strongly wed now. I found the strength in trust when reflecting on memories of my children when they were about five-year-old. At this age children face the world, for the first time, on their own, away from all the shelter we, as guardians, have provided them. They enter a classroom in a large school for the first time full of strangers, and we, the parent, walk out. Their mind recalls what we have taught them for years, "Never talk to strangers". When one thinks about it, a five-year-old child faces, larger than life, hurdles and challenges. It is through this journey of theirs, as they still hold what we no longer do, innocence, that their opinions really begin to develop and if one takes care to listen, one can learn from a five-year-old who shares their perspective on a world they are exploring fresh and new.

One Can Even Learn
from a 5-Year-Old

Imagine taking a seat in a classroom on the first day the of class. As everyone begins to settle in, the teacher, wanting to settle the class down, proclaims, "Everyone in this room will need to pay close attention to me throughout this class. You have everything to gain from me, and I have nothing to gain from you." I heard this once. Now, I am not sure that this quote is 100%, but the message is. This teacher clearly and sincerely felt that the purpose of the class was for them to provide knowledge to a group that had nothing to offer in return. When they asked the class if anyone had any comment in regards. I did, so I raised my hand, got called on. I remarked that one can even learn from a five-year-old if one is paying attention. The teacher laughed, and the class proceeded, though there was a felt acknowledgement of this truth in the room.

There are two points here. The first is to take with a grain of salt what you hear from an authoritative figure while in a learning environment, which is what life is, a learning environment. Do not fear to question what is said, explore, and verbalize your thoughts. Maybe, though, take care to articulate better than I did. Construct your opinion so that they are received in such a way to promote a positive dialog of further exploration.

Second pay attention to everything around you because the truth is you can learn from even a five-year-old. Sometimes, as we grow and mature, we can lose sight of the simplest of things that have so much importance, and the innocence of a child's remarks can help remind us of this. Also, they are now being raised in a society that changes much more rapidly than ours did. Their world does not mirror any like the ones before, so take note, as their challenges and opportunities do differ, and we can only help and learn if we are paying attention. Long gone are the days where children are to be seen and not heard. This is the world I grew up in. This old world did not foster and nourish our little beings. In today's world, learning and understanding all levels of the world around us, young, current, and old, is a great way to develop a voice that relates and adds value to the world that is developing quickly all around you.

Pay attention and develop your voice to the rapid world you are blessed to be a part of. Develop yourself in this space and speak maturely in it. Your voice is needed.

Speak up and be Heard
Your points not only matter, they are needed

Once, while applying for a new job, I was asked to provide references, which, of course, I provided. This time, the interesting part of this process was, when I was offered and accepted the job, I was also offered to review the feedback provided by my references. There was one which I was not exactly sure how to interpret. At first glance, I must admit, I took offense to one of the many comments from one of my references. While most of the comments were positive, there was one comment that I did not find to be positive at first glance. The comment addressed opportunities for my areas of growth and development. Not quoting exactly, but the comment mentioned that I am slow to speak up in meetings where members in the room believed I had much value to add. This came because I would not speak up when invited to do so. My reference shared that I have let those in the room down. Not a good thing to have your managers feel, believe, and/or say about you.

I reached out to this reference. I trusted him and was curious for more information about the comment he gave about me. He elaborated that my tendency to listen, and listen hard, during meetings, but not speak up and offer my thoughts, even if it was to say that I would like to time to further develop an idea that I had and would get back to them soon, left folks in the room frustrated with me. They would get frustrated because they valued and wanted my input. By not verbalizing a simple statement, even if admitting it was incomplete, I left folks in the room feeling deserted. I did not fully get this concept until I spoke, years later, with a trusted colleague who voiced the same frustration to me. I owe her a debt of gratitude for trusting our connection well enough to express and explain this to me further with a real-life example.

I see now that what I failed to realize before. I am invited into a room because my opinion is valued and if

I failed to deliver my valued opinion, or at least verbalize that it is in thought and being worked on, I am creating doubt against my own self in the room of my peers and my seniors. I have received this message and now I hold on to that lesson every time I walk into a meeting room where I have been invited. Old habits do die hard but I do make a conscience point to speak my mind now. If my thoughts are incomplete, I own that responsibility, verbalize it, and stand, without fear, in my shoes. I have started speaking my thoughts and that is value enough. I am there for a reason and I give what I can each and every time now. Being invited to the room does not mean do not speak up. Sometimes a question to clarify a thought in your mind is enough to get more experienced people thinking of something they have not yet thought to ask themselves. Value added.

Before the feedback, I failed to realize my value because I was carrying a past notion of myself, where I would believe that my ideas had little value until I fully developed that idea and brought proof of a concept with it. When I was brought up, if I did not come to the table with 100% proof, I could be faced with put downs from the person most relevant to the circumstance. The worse part about not speaking up was I also failed to recognize the importance of a team and the fact that invitation into the room was an invitation to a team.

"It takes a village", as the saying goes. It is time for me to quit fearing my role in the village. It is time you quit fearing yours as well. We are all here to deliver some importance in and to the village we are a part of and those new ones we are invited to be a part of. You cannot do or offer what others do. Just as others cannot do or offer what you can. That is the point! Step into your shoes and offer your village your voice. You are in your village for a reason. Take pride of your space. Your space matters. Let imbedded notations that others have ingrained in you go. Step into your shoes when you are invited into a conversation. Speak up and be heard. You have and are working hard for these moments. Be present and recognize when these moments are presented without the baggage of your past repressing your voice.

When you walk in your shoes, own and feel every powerful moment without offering power to the difficult, repressing past taking any ownership of your journey. Your shoes have taken you to a place where your points, not only matter, but needed. Receive the opportunities your shoes have brought you to. Your journey is well worth it.

Your journey is well worth it

Regardless of where you are today, you have journeyed. You have already taken steps in your shoes to get to where you are today. At points in your life, you have stepped into your shoes. If you feel that you may have stepped away from your journey, stepping back in your shoes is an immediate possibility. Your shoes are in your possession, always. You only need to give yourself your thought again.

Stepping into your shoes is not selfish. Someone must be you. Only you can be you. You are a needed being.

Accomplishing the things that you dream to accomplish are not impossible or impractical because you are not impossible or impractical.

Being the first you know to work on a dream does not make the dream impossible. The desire you hold deep is enough it for you to make it possible.

Speak up and be heard, one can learn from a five-year-old, take full responsibility, step out of the abusive relationship you may have with yourself, declutter and organize, seek the possibilities of your capabilities, map out your plan, incorporate you back in your life, make each day better, make connections daily – even the smallest matter, carve out time, remember that statistics do not define you, and most of all, know that, someone does understand!

Printed in the United States
By Bookmasters